the end of sepulchre street

Mark G. Pennington

Cyberwit.net
HIG 45 Kaushambi Kunj, Kalindipuram
Allahabad - 211011 (U.P.) India
http://www.cyberwit.net
Tel: +(91) 9415091004
E-mail: info@cyberwit.net

Printed at VCORE CONNECT LLP.

Contents

If you could take my bones

If you could take this mouth, and stretch it,
so that it fills the cornfields, so that it
moulds wax and makes honeycomb,
so that its saw-like tip can suck blood,
and it may tend to the flower nectar.
If these two curtains held taut could
let air pass, then it would say we have
roots in a bloodless brood, that we are not
strangers, that we are somewhere over the
haystacks, to caer mote and the shingle
of seascale.

If you could take these ears, and let them
listen, so that each note is pitched from a
clement scale, and the rising mist of that
secret horn has puttered into the language
of amnesty, and if we are pardoned then we
can liberate the fools, and if we can hear
the crack in those spoiled voices, then you
can hear the cry of a burdened man, then
let him holler until his satchel empty.

If you could take these legs, and let them
walk, so that each step is a print upon the
canvas, the key to a locksmith, a flower to
the honeybee, so that those hills may keep
singing, and if those pressings in the marsh
swim up as a carafe, rained and doused,
then take these legs with their crooked

bareness, their night hunger, their shallow
long goodbye, and walk with them until
the skin hangs with the rising rips of the
merciless tide.

And if you could take my bones then let
them plough earth,

rise up as bleeding
hearts,

kiss as hooker's lips.

Fishermen

Fishing with our crankbait under the shallow skin of a riverbend,
we sit as three on black rumpled tarps.
The day grows large, hunkered beneath oak and stirs of pondweed,
larger still until the sky bursts again.

The calm reeds that we see through the mizzle are butted by
the prow,
its nose like an unleashed, yet tempered cur.

We ponder who could leave such a beast untethered,
gently mocking the sounds of our trolling.

This boat could stand for anything, translating our telephone calls
or meeting in the misty peaks once snow-capped,
sodden in its underbelly.

I finger the tackle box beside the long grass,
nightcrawlers the slow bait from a miry land.
We wait for a strike in near silence but our hooks show no life.

The trees here are somehow different, they ought to be sleepier
than they are, if anything, they sing as loud as bellbirds.

And this sticks in my memory like a claw, that of the peace,
and pissing into the rain
under a can strung up to catch the butts.

We are novice fishers; we will not return to this place.

Upon the aft the tangle of reed and wet mud sits unfettered,
waiting for nothing,
just like us.

Running with scissors

A snowdrift lies across the ridges of my finger,
as though bleached by sunlight,
like hair with a teaspoon of oil to light the locks.

Its pale body grovels upon the skin, that which truckled
into blood under the sway of blade.

It was the scissors that made it, piercing cutters with
knife edge sharp as tacks.

It was in her hand when the moment came, another time
perhaps thought takes over, doesn't allow girls with
scissors to scurry around the classroom

like a runner on an ice skate tears at the verglas, then the
bitter flood pours out as a spindrift.
I am cut to the welt of blood, sprayed as scatter plot on
claggy, muted afternoon, and I turn to the window

where the rocks could topple at any moment,
I tell myself,
and crush the entire block, or so I tell myself.

The landscape harrowed by the wound I fly around,
poking the dim chemical lights with my finger bored in
another schoolyard bruise.

It is the release of a howl that haunts me just as
its ghostly shape now, stuck there in the narrow scores
of flesh like winter rain on crop.

It still reminds me of the first time a girl ever did
cut me to the bone, sharp-set for a brokenness that
drifts across the plain, snow-mouthed and silent.

No place like a home

I can see in its wintering esse, that the fieldfare
does cut from the dipper or the wren,

and I do not skulk in the undergrowth,
rather we sit on the high branches,
on the open bush.

I cannot claim joy in this homelessness,
among the tatters of wine, the smoke-clad
sofa,

but I am migrating of sorts, jumping between
the bark and the leaf,
leaping out of a drey, or the eyry struck from
mountain ranges.

That place once home has sundered,
broken, in disrepair, the tether sits at
the end of frayed rope,

and there is no place like a home.

But as the fieldfare sets its snow-capped quarters,
I too am picking the grass, twigs, nettles
to form the haunt that fits,

to dally in the west end, or hover in that special
Bayswater camp where her majesty of pancake
spreads her legs.

As the fieldfare can move, so I am given over to
the chuckling flock, and winter now where I lay,
upon this sofa, staring into the unhatched sky,

gather at the hawthorn hedge, the arable field,
mute as a dance.

A train for Katia

I can almost feel your hands now, wrinkling through the knots
on a sapped young back, tired and blown as Spanish cattle.
When you rub into *morillo* your hands are pulpous, softened to
ripe.

I often remarked this but you turn your head as a silent sigh,
face the mirror in that modest corner of Bayswater, and throw
all that sleeplessness to the opaque window - riled with last
night's rain.

A turbid sink rests playfully beside us, and in the mist of oil
I cannot help but close my eyes against the ember, silk
of your dress gnaws at my skin like rain on bone.

But there is a shadow here of her and him, the colour of your
hair,
sleek as satin, well clipped to the summit. I have brought them all
from the dinge to your ward.

As an apprentice to love I have shied with your lips spread in
hunger,
watched like a porter as you combed my hair, then as the wind
obtrudes to the tree, knocking all shape, I am forgotten.

When I took the train home I was blistered from your eyes, put
to
the grind again but for no more than a head full of rain, in a
dwam
before the storm.

The sculpted face of that night has pieces of me left behind, daring
to stroke at plush skin, roaring in the breach of the wind as it rips
through each leaf, one then two then three and I am gone.

All the horses

She is a walrus, fin-footed and slack with grief,
heartsick and dolorous,

she is hanging to the breathing hole.

She is a dog who would lay down whining and
take the jolt.

She is a fever running up the spine.

He is a minotaur, hand upon the deckle, wood pulp
in the stomach, ticks against the evening birdsong.

He is the wader bird, hunting tirelessly in mudflats,
waking against the stand, flapping and asleep.

She is a rodent leering to the jump, with chisel tooth,
packs the seed in her bag.

She is a walrus hunted for ivory.

He is over the stars, under the moon, around the sun,
he has a vat of pulp slurry from his fingers.

She is a teacher,

she hangs the song.

He remembers brightly,

he sings the song.

She is late summer cocking to the harvest,
mending the fruitless, temperate lag.

He arrives early as a rathe bird, by shod foot he
fences the greensward.

And of us we see the tether, the continuity of humankind,
the cord of life given

as if knowing all the horses in the field were to fall,
that they would make no sound.

The passing horse

Its black haunch is unmoving, set frigid under silver and soot.
Above its stiffened poll the chimney bunts that pocket of sky
but you can tell by the air that something is wrong.

It's the way the smoke seems to brood before arching to the
pall the sky has become.

Its body not asleep on the gradual slope turned to gate like
mountain to the runnel.

The single toe is caulked with muck, resting or deflated, a
stillness that gathers stride with menace
and cries at the sunbeam - a golden slip of lacquer on the
mare's hill.

The peace will be shattered when the body is discovered.
Its crest and withers stock-still, the barrel down and tail a
shiftless sagebud.

I was told stories of this horse, about how it bucked when it
saw fruit swelling,

pinned carrier and man to the stile, raced
over the fence in choler, and the wild years have gone to dust.

It is at peace upon that carpet of lea, still and unmoving,
yet it whinnies with those large eyes, those ghostly green sights
that I too can see with colour blindness.

It shall graze no more or wear that saddle, trot to the wire fed on carrots, lie upon that cut dried hay with sweet repose.

It is unmoving as I lean to the wall, grip my ankle in the space between stone and pry into the open air, heaving above its torpid bones.

I can almost smell the stench of death, the frowsty closeness that bitters in the wind,

then kiss the spirit so it can sleep, as hushed as mud, rested as stilly birds,
and run with the herd in the sky.

Cardiac arrest in the chip shop

It is high tide under the moan of gulls, starlings breach
the sky as the smell of cod nicks the air in Arnside's
muggy cleft.

The siren sounds with the rising bay and we are shuttled
into the back of land, cornered as rams with the shape of
sensing rain.

They bring him out down the narrow stairs - cramped and
reeking of vinegar, the uniform of paramedics like a ton
weight.

His purple face is starved of air, lips peeling over earthy
terracotta; gasping, he reaches to his tumefied cheek,
faint hand leering in the sunset

where the sky seems mute, hung iron blue over ambulance
waiting as sea urchin
with spiny cloth, tender heart.

We are told to move away, further into the searing heat,
we are also told not to look.
I snatch a stare at the crop fixing oxygen to his mouth,

see the blurred colouration masking his face, daring us
to ponder what will happen next.

I have seen the tincture of death before but couldn't phone
the ambulance and the helplessness comes back in swathes.

It is that moment of sitting on the front steps, quiet as
though no man had fallen, no sense of rain, only the echo on tv
of Jack Palance shooting Juno city.

This feels like we need to go home and call those who are
never far from the heart, tell them that whatever happens
in a lifetime

we can pair and preen as the finch with its hallowed bond
and let us stick like the orcas.

The man upstairs calls us one by one to collect our fish and
chips, and we go home riding into that Payne's grey of sky
feeling as though summer was finally over.

Morecambe Bay

Empty wagon blowing all that hot air, all that senseless noise.
A tongue sea-cracked, dressed as tarantula leg,

flapping like kelp below the Stone Jetty where the moon
left its teeth marks.

The empty, sallow moon biting like anglerfish.

In the sea I burrow there like sand rats.
I see the birthmarks on the seabed.

Those pressed against the bones of seaweed still dreaming in
amniotic sacks.

Morecambe Bay one Tuesday afternoon and effulgent stars
are laying upon the sea top, swimming like pansies or pure
diamonds - sopping with its glitter bones.

Sunlight upon the silken surface is a lover's rash, a coruscating
carpet
for small boats rocking in gentle hands,
reposeful sounds from a ticking harbour - like sea clocks beating
in
the rhythms of a new dance.

I arrive here as a mayfly with its eternal birth and when in the
sea
I am deaf as those forgotten hoary bones.

Morecambe Bay I see a slow teardrop inside your goldmine eyes.

And that wagon rolls by, the sibilant empty wagon,
empty for expelling all of its beautiful roses,

they drift to the saltmarsh and die for lack of care,
just like the footprints.

But before they perish, they prey on the ears of quiet heroes:
the listless sea bathers who can hear only the death of roses
among the seaweed.

The empty wagons are killing nature until it resembles
skin that has lost its elasticity.

Morecambe Bay send to me your graveyard flowers.

Therapy

He slips his shoulders back, leans into the embrace of the chair,
his eyes crowing behind the glass, as the morning cock.
I leap into the tiring air, make my indelible cuts in the skyline,
he casts a net.

This is the ungluing of thought, break of stone clutter,
I must tell him that to break is like walking through ice roads.

I sip at the tepid water and tell him that I know I am failing,
drifting further into the river, beyond the deep meeting distant
shadows of sun.

I can no more lift this mask to my eyes, or pretend here that
falling is my artistry.

Every word is shedding skin, undressing to the bone,
neatly as he scribes to the white sheet.

There is a file on me a mile high, inky and cumbersome,
holding the mire of my tongue.

I have given myself without a prize, turned to the mouth,
strung up the head, sat back in the deep
marrow of rebirth.

When it is over, he silently presses his glasses to
the skin of his nose, tucks a pen into his breast pocket.
It is the moment I remember most, the feeling
of emptying a bedpan.

The garden

She sits on her balcony watching over the tiered
garden.

The winds lash against fronds of fern, scattering spores,
its cool breath upon the toast and marmalade.

She looks to the misty heavens, tangled with skylarks,
and down to the pompoms that gather in arching sprays,
awaiting the whites of juneberry.

A vertical dogwood basks in the mid-morning rain,
missing the bold white bracts of summer, as does she,
and the unsung beauty.

It is the voices that steal through with trouble,
as far as the moon can show, they ring out
to the loneliest light.

She is helpless in her skin, that porous rock below
shows her the landing.

In this story she is yet to learn, all that she has is through
another's hand, the meltwater flitting through a
windswept garret,
then she asks the wind about truth, she feels an answer,
her conviction is as the grasses quaking gently in the breeze.

She thinks she ought to seek the wind in her hair,
wrap it around her fair skin, the helpless skin,
take it to the mountains and throw off the crown.

She has that place in her mind, barbed wire,
lost eyes, missing the whole summer, a chance at freedom,
but they never tell you about the aftermath.

Corn milk

The season was full spring and the air outside smelled
of corn milk,

as the record, with its tin whine, mewls
to a room of gunmetal and tub chairs.

Buggy talk layers the wetness of afternoons inside
redbrick, made by the kooks.

We sleep mostly, tethered to the papery bedsheet
as the mind with all that soil slowly grows again,
it will flower soon, if the bed is stable, if the
crown has taken to the mountain.

It will rise up as buckwheat full of mineral, lean to
the sunny side as perennials, the lupins or not so
crazy daises.

The food isn't great in the redbrick, tastes of refried
mush after dental surgery.

The skyline has that husk of blue settled on oaks,
willow shelters,
behind the barbs, over the water – you can see for miles.

You can see the peaks and crags, the snow tips
and the snowdrops, the roll of land that is as patient
as the oaks, the largo of which is defining its glory.

Someone always goes home, there is a line
that sings in the sweat of still life, that it will
be our turn soon,
that our time will come.

Spring rain

I pace the floor between the accent chair and the window

and nothing ever happens

until I replay that phone call.

I knew you were not here by the blossom
layering the cricket pitch.

It was the start of the moth bite in my cloth,
the ragged, empty moon shouldering the sky
as though it had never before seen the stars.

It was the moment when the maw refused
the fork, deciding instead to crack,
and then you were gone.

If I had let it ring inside the hollow breast of that hall,
ring so it muddied the air,
ring so that it cut up the pat of foot upon the wood,

then I would be sure that you are still here to propitiate
with prayer, to weave the darn.

In the bowl of cedar wood, cinnamon bark, mugwort,
you scented that air behind the cigarettes, the ones
which I threw to the ash pave

when you flex for the ground.

If that telephone had not rung with such turbulence,
then your grave had not salted, then your eyes not
cotton,

and withered as the sugarless freesia,

or silent in the boneyard yet to admire your grace.

But then you are gone in a phone call

not yet turned to wind

or worn as a hood against the spring rain.

The bartering

I imagine you gone, all of you, every piece bartered into dust
and not withered or shrivelled.

It is not slow as decaying flowers,

every bit sharp and hard as rustlers on a track, beaten by the
whisk of wheel.

Am I neurotic for imagining a death that has not yet
happened - for feeling the onrush of pain, the overhang of wave
threatening to drown?

And in that instance forgetting to revert to fish,
but witnessing the ageing of ourselves and knowing how hard it
is to smile.

It is 2 p.m. and I couldn't think of being anywhere else,

and how I would like to freeze time now, in this moment when
the
starlings come to drench in the bust of apples.

Why can it not be so?

I could scratch at the iron or paw at the sea and turn the tide to
beyond here. I could leap into the briar, set your ointment upon
the wound, turn back the clock.

One day it will be 2 p.m. and I won't be able to tell you,

and what?

That after four years a Sudanese woman was reunited with her
family,

that the arsonist gutted a church, and how they banded to form
their
service.

One day I won't be able to tell you and it will crush everything
inside
like a lung full of tungsten.

But I imagine it now under the silence of night-wash, sirens gush
down the street, I hear silence,

my ears peg to the speeding waul,
there is only silence,

a plangent cry that throbs in the heart of spring, I hear the
silence.

There is no way to halt the buck, prevent the ail or sore at the
needle,
still I cannot tow or grip the tiller,
as the quiet thought of you and not you rings loudest in the
bartering.

The sound of Gooseholme

If you stop, then listen, somewhere through the western gale,
at Gooseholme you can hear the purl and whirr of water,

the fall of running charge where swans canoe up its bend
quiet upon the famished limestone, the grikes awash and bled,

that it looks like an electric comb falling through the grey,
or the front grille of a Buick.

The runnel speaks too, of its seat at the guttural voice,
of its carpet to the fishers and eaters,

as the balustrade hangs with plastic bags, and they too scream
into the gale, rustling they flap unearthly as wraith.

The sound of rain comes like the bark of a broker's tongue,
lashes to the ground in currency if you hear it well.

Then the marching band will strike, a pelt of wind like
stone, hammer of rain to the back of our necks.

But if you stop and listen, you can hear the space between
lamb and mother, and the drowning that follows,

the earthen clod that sucks at frost, the ghost of
land, how it speaks through birds, how it curls as smoke.

If you stop and listen, you can hear the breath of everyone
who tried to keep the flood at the gate,

and fell into marsh, lived upstairs, shouted and screamed
at the wall, but if you listen hard then you can hear

the storm-bitten bridge, the ruins of nature's war, rumbling
against the backbone of a verdant sod.

Water

This water is hungry, it is a landing strip,
it echoes into the bank with a yomping parade.
Grasses lay at her changing face; birds drink her lifeblood.

A mirror for geese, cackling, irradiant,
underneath the blazing screw it sets out a corridor,
a litter of light as the crow flies.

Water is the child who left his baggage in your womb,
learnt that they take miles off you,
would kill you given the chance.

It pulled down bridges, retired them, took
homes away from churchgoing folk, we
gave our plastic and cigarettes.

Clear as the mountain dew, keeps photographs and
the echo from mudslide fells.

Empty egg crate lay soft in its wandering,
grey artless shell. Soon night draws in and stops
these whispers of dead relatives.

This water has been heard, is not hard of hearing,
has been heard in the great lakes and meres.
Hear it tonight on your rococo balcony,

the awnings brought here in 1950, water heard
them all. It fed the fisherman and crept up the
door, unbroken, sleeping.

The dusk's last hurrah

It was the fear of spiders first, the way their tree-like legs
would flicker,

bast of which hunts at the plaster wall, magnified in
silhouette by lamp shine.

Then it was to wash the stems of roses, my arms around
your waist, water plashing from a tired basin.

The pears from a tree in the neighbour's garden that would
not be stolen, when there was such a thing as neighbours

and even they were bad.

Earlier there was not to eye the sunset close enough to
powder us with stardust, leaving the rings of fire, then that
sunset would not leave at all,

and we have dreams,
dreams that can be disinterred one morning without a
voice, willing from that place where you are not for I have
only dreamt your death.

It is the recipes that burl through ourselves, sticking to the
wood that becomes us.

It is in the bleach that your face cannons like a speeding
rocket, tearing through sky at the dusk's last hurrah.

It was not just a thatch of hair, or the cup of Burmese eyes,
the dimples on the cheeks, but a waft of endless things

only you could tell,

a pocket of water slowly emptying as the sun sets over the
roof,

then into the pudgy night stars named by the sulk of moon as
it carpets your pillow

and in the dusk's last hurrah you mend the broken, tin gods
and lowlifes,

weaving as a mother who sewed the moon to the sky.

Gutter birds

In growing thinner, the morning has sucked its birds
into the gutter,
and they each wet a pointed wing and sup with beaks
from round heads, cadging a mud-lined nest.

As the sun of its eye ring ensnares the wet as a springe,
it submerges in this bath or ewer, makes pretty sounds
with its fluted warble,

or chink and chook to caw away the cat's sinful wait
where it is an immotile doll at the foot of the door,
hunger in lucent eyes, watching threshing wings.

The blackbird has found its bosom, from the tree where
a river bathes its sunken root to the hop into gutter.

When the windows slam shut, for breath has cooled that
room, cat arcs stiff, live as tethered wire cut loose, frantic
in its searching sting.

The birds carry on in their sluice, slaking whatever
troubles they seem fit.

Then as sun held up like a pear in a tree, gathers its
calefaction, winds the motor, and spells the drift to
afternoon with slow dance behind the chimney.

In that moment I have seen the great affair, where hands
can be feathered, noses beaked, and mouths quiet,

'cept only for the melodious chink that saves us from
the belly of the beast.

The sound of tears

I would leave a pot of steak on the stove then go
work the production lines,

night quilted as lampblack soot, cold and starless
yet rankled by sweat,

sigh with the pulling of bath sheets and napkins,
place them in the wrong
carts sometimes to hear the flurry of Polish.

Once there I would think about the girl at number
five and how she needed the rain to fall through
her street tears.

She wanted to go to hospital but they kept telling
her that it was better to learn to dance in the rain.

The sound of rill bleeding through stone when it
did rain meant she could cry with company,

and leave the night fruit to wither into scalding
jellybag, oily and scented of turpentine.

At the maw of night she would caw into the sett
she had dug, my work boots thundering

the stairs as sallow moon paints the wall
above the door,

an image which reminds me that sometimes tears
are no good unless they are the fallen leaves on
a hardy autumn night,

the leaves falling with breath like the huff of
a handgun.

I knocked on her door just to offer my shoulder
or anything at all, but she smiled instead of puling
and then said she was fine,

with a lilt that sang as the great veery,

she simply and quite wonderfully said,
it's the rain you see:

it always gets me down.

Dear diary

In those last two years she was known as the girl who tried to kill
herself.
Wearing felt that wrapped those burdened,

sinking shoulders. A lamb into
the river or as pallid sun stretches out, broken and watered.

Dear diary, this has to be the moment we never forget, I wrote.

As the lunch hall would inflate like gas in a balloon, she waited at
the
shutter screens later than us and mute and alone.
Although I don't think

it was always that way.

Just before that happened, before that stretching for the rainbow,
a boy was almost unplugged from his life support.

It was a strike of wood at the corner of the head, splitting from a
cutter,
sharp and quick in a coma.

In my diary I drew the pills and the shutters,
and me alone by a tree.

We must remember this, I wrote.

And how could we forget?

We would pass then in a sweaty corridor as the threads hung
from
her breasts,
jeans so dirty they smelled even at distance, torn and faded
like a summer storm.

I would nod at her then, and somehow felt that it was better, as if
my
haircut had powers to strike out depression,

dear diary, I have strung up the cow and am now attempting to
pick
daffodils for the use of bookmarks.

How lonely can it get when you're stuck at the
bottom of a feed bag?

This is true, I wrote, and I would much rather be cynic
than an ashtray.

I wondered how her lips tasted,

when she would make the end of sorrow.

Whether she could see where the ocean goes to sleep,
and how she would wear it on her rubescent cheek.

When we all graduated at the ends of a lost and bitter love,

she smiled,
not once, but twice.

Dear diary, I can't thank her enough.

On the green

The girl lived across the road, orange string hair
shaped in a bob and pebble dash freckles,
guzzling a pint of milk
on the return from the corner shop.

I can break in and see you in the shower, she said.

This was all on the green, seemed joyous back then,
freshly cut and sprouting young dandelions, sporting dew
like sweat on a horse's mane.

I watched her eating soup in the downstairs window,
smiling as I made faces. Anything to make her laugh.
We sat on stone walls and kicked footballs back and forth.
We made a den in the back garden, our hovel of timber
helmet against the lash of rain, practised kissing, both
on lips and dock leaves.

Often, she had a mouth full of language
belonging to the sewer, or the scaffolders
at yards where wolf whistles plough the dirt.

It all seemed to be a part of growing up.

Her tales of sexual conquest make me smile now,
just a bit of in-out, like some clockwork orange lady.

She moved away one winter and the German lady
on the corner died.
The Wests went too and so did their garden.

New houses were built, new worlds, new dens.
I wonder what she would have made of the mud mountain
that sat in the corner of the green, now turning old.

Passing through Bowston

As the winter sun glimmers in mist and clouds
like a torch through the bedsheets, the sheep
graze in the field, full as afternoon shoppers
in their bargain threads.

I walk in the rain through Bowston, passing a
window gummed with the scent of an oil heater.

It is cold and it reminds me of our old house,
especially the empty coal shed with its missing
bricks, just like infants with gaping dark holes
where there should be front teeth.
There used to be a railway line, I am told.

When I reach the fields, I have already trodden
through woods singing of wild garlic, bluebells
and liverworts.

I am reminded of my fear of lying amongst the fern,
wet mulch of leaves and mud crawling through my ear,
the creeping of spiders and ticks.

I am a city man I think, but there is something strange
about the scent.
It longs for company, to share its music.

In the vast plain grasses, cows stare with their
open hearts, they are right to distrust usually, not

this time. I walk gently as though on foreign legs,
an intruder stapling his footprints to the lifeblood.

I peer to the hills where an avalanche could come down
at any moment, as if the fringe might topple over and
crush everything down below.

The horizon belts out under the grey fog, a thread of
green pinning together the chaotic sky.
It is full of a secretive film.

The painter

Stood at his easel, mid-morning light;
the train tracks are still warm, but I am
not a guest of that carriage. Not that
rickety beast that wheeched the sky
and set green arcs to clay.

Here I have turned to find a meaning,
an answer.
His feet are bare and soundless
on the hard floor, mottled with paint.
There are no secrets out there, he says.

His shins still ache from the landing,
war tears flesh, but he knows he is
ready for anything.

He knows I am lost. The spring has
bucked and tempered, allowing infant
seeds to drink from a rain that dapples
threads.

He hands me a notebook and asks:
What did the little boy want to be?
I plucked the paper and wrote it instantly,
in one breath, one word.

He strokes the canvas with a brush
and a part of me has hatched.
I imagine living a life unburdened,

birthed to cross a border with no sentry.
Free as the language itself.

He dabs at the drips on his clothes
and the goldcrest pecks at seed upon
the window sill
as I turn to answer.

An old dog called Flint

Walney Island glisters and rings in the sunset.
The sand sits at low water, brushed by icy fingers of the Irish
sea.

We watch the dog chase away gulls
on west shore beach.
But he stops every time the distance becomes too great.
Almost like there is a tether between us, an unseen bind
roping together all that matters.

Some see him bow-legged, or scared to move with those
well-hidden yet furrowed brows.
He limps from time to time because his leg was broken,
set badly, whether he was racing or his poor bones -
but he is a rescue, so the answers are missing.
Flint by name and flint by colour.

It becomes his crutch for when he no longer wishes to walk,
or when he can no more, just a sounding bell and
we don't know if it has been heard before.
His worried eyes tell us that he doesn't want to be alone,
not now after the charity, the manumission.

When he sleeps, he makes contact body to body, his warmth
beside the inglenook is a nest, and we huddle.

Now he bounces along the beach, giddy, and starts to totter.
Barks at the wind like an old poet.

The water carries small stones and silt and clad; he watches with a fascination seldom seen.

As we crunch among the shingle, I feel it too, the unseen bind, measuring every second for its fame.

Morning flight

i

We set off in the dead hours,
coloured by night's hunger.
The crepuscular animals are like sirens in the sky
and the roads are quiet, still as oil portraits.

My nerves are creeping into the red,
overloading my sense of peril.
But airports do this, even when they are empty
as John Lennon is this morning.

I had to drink wine this morning just to get into the car.
Its sweet plums leaving damson sugar on my tongue.

We check the bags and thankfully they are carried on,
we watch them as we might a child untethered.

I can't eat but welcome the coffee like that
old medicine my mother used to give.
I even think of my departing words to her now.

The thrust from the jet engine propels our
huge craft into the far reaches of a dusky blue sky,
spilling the tenebrous cloud below like scattering
breadcrumbs along a carpet.

It is not how I remember it.

Crossing the ocean bed, I try not to think
of our graffiti in the deep blue below. But what if I never get
back home? More pressing is what will I be remembered for?

We touch down on foreign land at last, see the sun that looks
different
now, alien, that much more torrid and claggier.

ii

The bicycles of Amsterdam rest against their backbones,
the trains carve through river and green, sheets of
traffic almost collide in the mess, fusing footsteps
and tyres together.

The flight is still running in my veins,
even though the cathouse is beckoning
me forwards with a vacant charm,
one seldom seen back home.

We are eating sugar bread in the street, dipping
churros, listening for the heart of the city,

inside the brown café that carpets the table,
the panorama, the crowds
of Vondelpark,
all things one does in another clime.

The city zips by and leaves the taste of
jazz in my mouth.

Beyond Betty Blue there is a girl wanted
sign, marijuana with its gooey eyeball
litters the street and I eat my breakfast
without the tails of England lapping at
my throat.

I almost become a native - my tongue,
still wine-bitten, adopts the Dutch accent,
without thought,
one less tail lapping.

After the flood

The wet-down came in torrents, lashing and bleeding
over fragile earth,
bucketed against the limestone.

It was the sight of furniture on lawns - the sweeping
of water away from garden gates, dowsed carpets
fit for the fell – that sobered in the aftermath.

The floods were the worst in a lifetime,
only it was not so rare we were later to
discover.

Winter's aqueous grip held tight over us,
our grey town.

The laved green and grey, the miry paths,
the roads borrowing from rivers turned to
muck palettes with no respite for livestock.

Trees are now at the mercy of our defence,
the hewn of bark felled like summer in the endzone of May,
but the rains keep coming.

We wait again and again, trusting in sandbags,
watching the river become a glut - the torrents
that won't relent -
spilling its insides over the bank.

The chaos of rain befitting a modern tragic play,
sorrow painted the colour of bust rivers.

After the flood we go on living,
hang the bird feeders, cut the grass, mend to
the washing,

tell our stories to the children, wondering if they
will remember in another lifetime.

Easy living

This bed is gentle, soft, rocking. I am in utero. I lay upon the
white ship,
the sheets lap at my beard, easy living in the morning,
easy in the afternoon.

The bed is tied to my hair, it is knotted in a conch shell,
it tethers me and licks my wounds.
Throughout all the alarms it warms me, pulls my arms into the
centre of its cave.

It is quite easy being depressed. It is quite easy.

I see the cats on the lawn all depressed.
Imagine a world without cats, it would be like no mirrors.
I watch the footsteps of the rain, hear its pattering against the
window,
another day another dead dream.
I wanted it to rain.

I want it to rain, rain, rain. I ache for it to rain.
Then I cannot move.
I cannot help but steer this ship to quiet, to lonesome.

Through the dark I rub at the wool that is taped to my wit.

Now the waves speak of skies without its sunlight, my disappear-
ing youth,
louder and emptier, then rain and rain and rain.

This is easier than running or bending knackered joints, greater than pleasing
a mass of cocksuckers.

It is easy to fall against the sea and be carried.

This dark mountain range under a bitch moon, sleeping now as babies,
warm in the drifts, swallowed up.

They say nothing matters, nothing at all,

either that or everything does.

Wold cottage

We drove beyond heather-covered moors,
windswept dales carved and shaped by ice
with a festive surfeit of booze idly rattling in the boot.

We almost gate-crashed somebody else's quick getaway,
the road not being too clear, a path winding and
grass-specked, hidden in the furrows, dipped between bark.

When we unpacked, we were greeted by a gyre of
houseflies at the window – the conservatory that would
be my nook for the week.

I let them out and took down to the beach,
the shingle that runs along a narrow spit
of land.

The children tore apart the breath in the air, but
at this time of year is there anything purer?

It was a view I hadn't expected.
One in the sunniest December I had ever seen.
The great lush plains of greenery cropped to the bone,
vacant and bountiful to the very ends of the horizon.

It seemed to live on forever, perching ground for
the crows, brambling visitors, redwings.

In the brilliant white of that room I took morning
gracefully as I could, as if it were my first,

the lyrics of a song nailed up in the bedroom never
leaving my side plate of coffee, staining what looked
like shale.

At the table, which you laid with skill learned
passing through that Spanish quarter, we sank
the wine and pulled those crackers,

plucked bread from a creel, always rooted to that
gravel land outside the sea of windows.

River Kent

The night's wind gulders and howls, rain buckets -
sheets down, trapped in the sill's ridges.
Hail plummeting, the moonstone to earth like fireflies
in the sallow lamplight, each carrying their death.

I live on the river, at the edges of this grass runnel -
the vitreous, silvery metal of water buried in the delf from Bela,
if you follow its snake hide far then at Winster you hear the echo.

The sprout of reed – a nib flowering gently, motile
in weathered stone like a grass birthed in the fat of bird
feed – pockets a gem from the stone base.

The river makes its music on a damson bed, a sparge
of glitter dabs at the pores and rain sheets to the glass skin,
this roan-haired inlet sucks it up,
transports to contours through waterfowl.

On this night the moon with its shard of dusk has swum in the
sweat of the river, painted moonstone on its snake hide and
suspired against its silk.

The weekend canoes that drift beyond
the window are in debt to this water, as is the fowl,
as is the child, as is the fisherman, as is the knoll
with its splendid view.

I rearrange the daffodils so that I can see
through to its sendal skin, catch the whites
of riot running along, sometimes carrying
a bough from the birch.

Maudes meadow

It is more of a path to someplace else now,
not the garden it once was; a rickle of leaves
where the wood shack stood.
The cornflower out, as the cowslip and primrose
make way for more seating, a backbone ripped
with the hooded youths' transhumance.

The winter sun cups can no more be laid,
as the ground levels to that of a plankway.

There are no more corners to hide,
the open plan makes it bare as cropped wheat.

Nothing to hide behind, not that we need it, but
we like a busy nook full of blue butterflies and
bellflowers, the musk and florals of the sweat of
daffodils, the closeness and the intimacy,
body abutting land.

It had a tree once where a cane abutted its trunk,
around the floral beds it grew wide and tall,
then the sound of grandfather's voice would
shake its leaves, give in to kites and
birds like the corncrake from Skelgylll woods,
the nuthatch from Walla Crag.

It had an overgrowth, runners and foliage
unperturbed yet as loud as the clicks of
whales.

It was our place then, on the towels
and the sunscreen, bathing in its
cabochon, gently hawing at the sun trap
and its favourite meadow.

Daffodils

The first time you see them dead it sinks your
heart, a heart once propitious, sanguine,
anchored already at nadir.

The ones you've tended and watered and grown,
watched day to night to day,

would sniff its musk, innocence, sweat and
watch the sun dance upon its core, its bone
until open and with stretched limbs search the
sky as in a fever.

It plants the seed of grief, hardens the body.

The hills with their half-moon bow setting
the arc of life, ever organic with the organs
of a Malvern postcard, while the daffodils
rest their weariness upon a naked moon sill.

The first time you see their death it withers
something all the way to the soul.

Take them into the trash and watch as the flower
becomes a soiled tissue,
or an empty carton, a glabrous twinkle of stardust.

It goes on that tether, it goes beyond the
watch-mate or the cultivator.

It goes on until more life can be grown, birthed like
new children.

If you hold that crumple of petal you can still feel
its incredulity, gently stinging the strands of still
life until there are no more moons to be hung out
like bed linen.

No more mountains sluicing the downward spiral
of earth.

Hatful of odium

The refrigerator in that dead night is a canvas starved,
it hums with the buckling tymbals of a cicada, eyes
just as wide, as cryptic, and its mechanical mania
as musical.

It is for the lack of sleep that I hear, that I feel
from its ribs, that good repose is absent as dreams.

I walk onwards in that dead night under a carpet
of brittle stars, moonlight creeps between the mill of grey
cobbles, the river in spate covers the berm now
watery and pitched as a muck bath.

If I walk further in this cold moon, to waterside and to
the river's bend, I can barely make out the night's dusky
arc of hill, where the mare
kneels to the turf, staggered and blown.

That dead night is long, ponderous, laggard -
if you will, but the acid that comes with sleep
is most unwelcome.

I can water my dry mouth in those late bars, where
there is too much smoke, too much noise, and a night
crowd that feels hard and unjoyful.

I can stand at the jukebox wearing my sullen
eye and my hatful of odium.

I must leave and make tracks in the furrow,
for I cannot bear to hear any more ringing
in this night dust,

the breath of the wind malefic and serious,

this ongoing watercourse building to
a bank of soft earth.

The bells are ringing

The sun caked over the low hills, from the
Howgill gritstone and on the Lune through
the ruins of Parr castle,

it gleams with a dancing flare between
those sheltering yards,

and on the knoll where the sole tree props up a
wintry stippled sky,

there is a bounty of grass wet from the whisper;

that fat sun has gorged until it watered from its
brutal, whiskered mouth.

In auld grey town the paths are closed to visitors,
even in this spring sun that rips at the threads of
a latch, a gate to the lakes no more.

This place has become a mollusc, shut off in the
sand, starved and laved in a sun wish,
as grazed sward hungers.

The touch of man has scattered sour moods all over
this plain, among the marsh and moor,
the mire and the meadow,

it has been rung far from here as the death toll
rises and the stars are milk drops.

The bell has sounded its death march, from hammer
to clank, and of all the things I miss it is the tread
of foot upon the familiar,

the hustle of streets made foggy by the sheer
weight of number,

the welt of each step, coming together as one.

Gentle night

after Dylan Thomas

We lost him late in the falling tears of autumn,
and like a shredded leaf, a perished bottle of
vodka, we witness the dark decaying.

At the funeral we heard the cries, the song
stuck up with a northern wit, feathered by
congruity.

A man has drunk him into the grave,
we see only the shatters of what left behind,
the shape of music to come.

If I were to curvet toward the summer,
back beyond the still flowers, weep then
I shall put down the pannier, share the
wishbone, rest against the bust.

When the stories flutter about the room,
nobody tells of the murk, the long kiss
or the silence of a tenebrous,
unspoken line,
the distance between love and loathing.

On this day it seems impossible that you
should part, not without licking the pages
of a magazine yet to be turned,

or feel the tendril of an orchestra gently blowing
in through the speaker.

It is the lasting image of a trig and happy
man holding up the Mediterranean sky that
follows me around, throughout the
churchyard and the hanging trees, it sleeps with
me at the court of dreams.

In an instant there is one more hacking into
the stew, this rumpled tarn,
praying to the angel,
and that night has sung its last,

the cold quietus sloping down the runnel,
and then good and gentle night.

Naked in the ruins

This burdened man comes by with a light, tells me it is not
my fault; he says that I didn't deserve it, and that I've
been there.

He carries with him a broken saddle, and when I look to
the omen of those real swallows,
I see the darkness above heads in a stitched grey blanket.

He has a rum, queer old way to him, as if the present was
the most important thing in the world, yet he often regales
of those millwright years.

With his moon and his spade, he digs so that we can see
him in the trench.

Then to that place that has my thorn,

I carry the broken noose like a tail,

I thought I'd left it at the staples in those bob wires, where
the cattle rot through their eyes.

I am trailing it behind my step, brushing at the ends of the
curb, lashing at a plashet sick of footsteps.

That darkness gathers at the nib of spitlers edge, combs
down the slope,

it follows me as I ask those whispers in the wind to cease,
and what you hear is only for you.

I can still hear the wretched, joyless cry of the crows, circling
the sky scoping out carrion, or leading above the battlefield.

They never leave the tops of trees, those that scream naked
in the ruins of the priory.

The clothes basket

Wednesday morning the Japanese soldiers came, muddy
boots, red sash belts tied for luck, the shin gunto – a
sword of death, shining like pearl of moonlight in a river's
distended mouth.

The children had long stopped playing on Creek Street
when grandmother was fifteen and a half.

Walter and father had taken a broken gramophone for repair,
their inerrable footsteps chattering in the fog,
a boy scout uniform winking with a furtive charm.

Then the soldiers brought them to a halt.

When grandmother saw the bruises, she reached for another
cigarette,
a comfort that would last over time.

When the Japanese soldiers came grandmother hid in the
clothes basket
and the children had long stopped playing on Creek Street.

Those prayers started here, grace and goodnight,
amongst the screams
of planes above, those awful blasts, the machine guns – stuttering
through the bowels of the long night.

Grandmother was afraid to sleep in case she couldn't hear the
sirens.

They returned one time to piles of dead, dust, and rubble.
Auntie had not made it through.

The soldiers left, a house upturned, but grandmother was safe,
she was hiding in the clothes basket.

Now she removes the mask giving her air, the morphine drops
to the hard floor, she needs it for the pain.

She strains through cataracts, leaves a hand hanging by the
bedside.
Those prayers ring on through ceremonies of new skin

and she sings her Burmese song, still she lives the stories,
especially the one about the clothes basket.

The shoe factory

Here at Gallowbarrow, the shoes are stacked in
ordinary grey boxes, steeped to the roof.

Summer has broiled and raddled the skin,
this begrimed factory is walled with crud,
the windowless hue of tar.

The dust, thick and black and dirty, fills my nose but still I sweep,
endless strokes across the stone, as the weight of bones crawl
upwards along a slope of scree.

This brush can be used as a leaning post under the
black dust.

I sit upon the ladder, this metal stair, wasting hours
as only not listening to evening birdsong
can be – especially in summertide or rainless days.

It is a far cry from reading Catcher in the Rye in the campus bar,
professors extolling or to dive in puffery.
The smell of ale and musky ink, Hilary term already
full of birth – the parturition.

Now the sunny season grips nations in a vice,
taut and toothed like a hack, we are
clamped as Denver boots in the high altitudes.

But why must I quit?
Groucho Marx has perhaps said it better, but is it

because I do not want membership of a club
that has me as one of its own?

My hands have nimbly picked before and folded like cards,
quicker than the rest, unwise and honest.
Here though the whip is unseen and partisan for the native.

They will work here until retirement, never guessing
blue collars have sipped at a sunrise less tepid than
resting breakfast tea.

Then one day they are gone, shut off from the sea,
rudderless, without anchor again.

Autumn song

The autumn comes with its mercurial music,
sheeting down the crags, the Old Man, peaks
turning to their snow-capped underbellies.

It sings with its barley and fire, shoots arrows
and bows at the window where we sit as barren
fishermen.

I climbed the hill with my bicycle, my boyish heels,
sucked at the sky and felt it move.

I gave it my salt lips and mouse hair, then the sky
larked and bent downy wings into flight.

I stood at the tips and peered down to the tops of trees,
green as artichokes and coriander.

Fear left me and I was lifeless as the promise of
death comes with its own song.

The pulpy land lay below, my teen kicks unbridled
at the gazing.

I wanted so to taste the earth, minerals, water, air.

I wanted to drop like sun rays and feathers,
feel the whip of the sky lashing.

It was the voice of the wild that found me.

When I leapt into the wind, I heard my heart
cowing against the ferine mouth of coyotes.

I wanted to sing.

I wanted to scream the song loud.

I landed on hard, uneven ground, stony, patchy, burnt green.

My leg twisted and bruised, crumpled under my own weight.

I gazed up to the trees, the billowing cloud, the plumy sky,
I closed my eyes. I wanted to hear the wild.

The anthem calling me to sing.

Orchestra of the night river

It was you facing those rolling hills,
you as peat as earthen

and smog,

beneath the yellow bricks of the county hotel,

your back as strong as spider's silk, tongue as
weak as onion skin.

You were at the station, a film of shadow,
an oil slick, a mute actor,

lonely and famished upon that night-washed stone.

All along the canal path you came striding
as if the
bounty of that stripe was near.

When you turn around

but you don't turn around,
you never turn around,

and that darkness hangs on silver birch
as it droops to the floor,

tissue paper of its white bark hungers,
the touch rough but it waits,

it held its breath for you.

You were there on the platform in that ink and jet,
as the gorse seemed to wither,
mute against the running train.

If it stops here and waits then it would see
its fair rose county shed feathers and stand
to the night

like a watchman,

silently waiting that she should turn
and turn
and turn

until the moon of that mean sky starts to sing,
louder then with its dusted wane,

still hidden by the orchestra of the night river.

It was you then and it is you now,

your neck a dancehall,
your thighs unbridled; you seem to be silent still as the
land waits and waits,

for you to turn around, to see and
to hear the summer bourn,

the trouble pouring out of a heart laying into the loam,

standing not three feet from you.

Notes from a birthday book

For all the things you could not save, but a lock of hair
pressed to the clip, a set of earrings so small they can
slip down through the eye,

and of her tale with those courageous enough to leave,
of the water and light,

the bomb and the ladder, her handbag which had all
of life's chattel.

Here is an address book which began, Jesus bit O sunshine,
a hymn I could never have heard
but there is a tear that wells for every day in that cage,

the pocket mirror which cradled the moon, stuck on
your lipstick and held the sun as a baby.

My photograph in headshot five times, carried in
your bosom-like nest, sidled against the soft skin of you,
my photograph in ruins now,

for that face is not living, that it died with you.

Those earrings were wrapped in tissue, as it would be
taken up the sleeve,
carried as bird eggs.

Then a tattered slip emerges from that well,
a wedding photograph scarred by the whites of eyes.

We all know it now, stoic man,
resplendent woman addressed to ma and pa,

the olden grey rivered by tulle veil and starry tulip.

Then a little elephant comes out of the bag,
I can only imagine your bearing of the children
who called,

of your sense of humour and
your height.

You grow like Bugbanes.

In the pages of that book you call on us
to see the inner stone and flower,
the granite of our make.

Mine was opal and calendula, you said,
yours was diamond and sweet pea.

And then you sign off, a language written
by your hand, a tall way of seeing
that shine as you say love lights the path they tread.

And then you are gone again, leaving the stars
to shed their mystery,

the moon to become overfed and dance at the
sky's edge,

when only the contents of a handbag mean the
whole of the universe.

Wither at dawn

I am lost, I cannot find my way, my route is a blackened thorn,
blinding tar.

My legs hover and drift up toward my chest, the ground is
marsh and I can't move,

there is no gravity here.
I am leering to the mammoth air above where I float like
apples in a basin.

There is a house with a garden, and long, wiry reeds stubbornly
erect sprouting from the soil.
I know it yet I can't name the living or the dead here.

Now I am grounded at last, but fear something from the
house that becomes more shack and ramshackle as time passes.

It is farmland, I am sure now that I smell those pigs.
Only it is not like smelling, more like feeling.

As my body roots, I feel the sorrow cry of
something repeated, not a warning but a memory buried
that aches to come to the surface.

I know I am a child here as the lens stands at the tip of
those reeds, unsteady and afraid.

A voice beams through the trough where the water swims,
as the pigs start to snuffle, a warm brew
hanging from those snouts like ice off a roof gutter.

It says to me these words: David's son talks like the pockets
of Aristotle.

And I was a dropout, I was lost, I could not find my way
and this was not in the dream.

There is a place, or rather places, that I left behind, my eyes
at the train station, my ears in the hollow corridors of a
university, my mouth at the bar,

my heart with a fair young girl who rode horses on pasture,

but this was not in the dream.

If they are premonitions foreboding, memories dissolving,
an impulse, a repressed wish
they are what they are,

but if they are another self, living another life, allowing me to
glimpse its riches and direst message,

then it is all lost as blossom will fall through the window,
scutter in the sink,
snap under the sudden crunch of my weight.

The night has brought its beauty, with wraiths and manes,
and dreams are the strangest of creatures.

A dream like blossom raining through the street,
withering at the dawn.

The cemetery

Even though dusk had arrived we could still
hear the birds calling

out through that willow nest,
the branch alive with tangled ostrich feathers,
or it was the black plumage of garbage bags,
shredded, flapping in the wind.

We glimpse the scut of rabbit chasing darkness
around the headstone,
then silence which was almost death speaking,
had we been trenched into battle yet again?

An ornery sky, gently weaving through billows
and furrow, threaten tears that cuff the living,
a pat of prints from their flowers digests the
humas

where it lay, but there is green to be devoured.

Grass is not yet shaved but for bathers
it is glorious, underneath willows and garbage,
the plumy overhang.

Ceremony lasts in its ghostly form, the wight
sailing across our starry night, old grey weeping,
vibrating at the cheekbones

as a hushed hillock leans to
the stone wall.

At the grave where you lay a cry salts the sheen
upon your stone,

and it is in giving that we receive.

Prayer and song often wound together, roped
between the singer and the kneel,

and it is in pardoning that we are pardoned,
it is in dying that we are born to eternal life.

Then back to that little room on the river we stay
awake on ginger and scotch and douse those memory
fats in warmth,

we seek to see the wraith of you walking with your
frame away from the callow light and onto a form
that sings more like ghosts than you.

We see the wool of your cardigan nightly,
the smell of red lentils, onions cooking in a skillet,
brews of old houses with holes in the stairs,

there you travel and avoid the morning as the rush
hour traffic brings you back.

Flint at the morning rain

Put down the leg and lie upon your roost,
eyes of burnt umber closing,
teeth gasping at the air as wild reed from riverbed,

flint hair bubbling with lumps,

and if the snap of a case as shutter screens in a
diner pollute the sleep; you hide in the next room on an
unmade bed,

bletting at the eye of a hammer, flinching at the
risen bell,

harrowed at the morning rain.

The cancer never leaves so a snap sharp as box cutter,
or a fallen pen is sudden shock.

Outside there is your soiling lawn, where a war for
apples nearly sent you away, racing through the garden
on ratty legs your rat tail bitten as orange seed

and the apples fall like drunks.

He sees the bird at the fountain, drinking as from a ewer
and he wants the bird, he wants to be the bird mockingly
scudding through the skyline.

It may be no more than a hospice,
sleeping together as brown bats, seal brains working to
stay afloat,

but your clean jaw looks strong in this light, where masts
are drawn from Grayrigg and through the shipyard,
to home, to your roost, then sleep.

Things I wish I'd known in 2002

Don't hang in one place like the mist or the moon that
flowers on the lonning, it stills like cold water, draws
the mayflies.

Try to feed the birds as often as you can, the song will
bloom like the reddest rose, but scatter the seed to the
lawn, the grass grows better there.

Don't refuse the bike on Golden Gate Bridge, leave the
prints of sand on your feet, the bay hangs clearer in the
dew left behind.

Be gentle with time and don't obsess over waste, this
includes time.

If you can cultivate for the growth of flowers, then you
cannot be wary with the heart, and give it in scads
and oceans. If it is true then give it.

There is a weight in regret, but don't allow that to be
the reason for not hustling.

A street can be a mean place, take the comfort of strangers
when it happens.

There is a want and then there is a need, understand the
difference.

Give the night your attention for these are the working
hours, always see the tears of the Langdales

and then be the one who laves in the welling of the rain,
for you will smile often and no flood will corrupt.

Take the scenic route.

Do not listen to the cries of madmen, they have gardens
that mirror chaos, they will never be sated.

Be at one with the stars for usually they have only the
wings of crickets.

Don't flatter death as it has too many hands on the wheel,

also forget the tumult that you served, there is greater
meaning in catching fish.

But no lesson is a bad lesson.

Don't stay in the same crowd, however much they
feel like home. It is not always best to root without
chance.

Listen to the rain, it is often the most beautiful music
ever composed,

and trust in intuition,

and make blood concrete.

There will always be a rise of bluebells where witches
make their brew,

but throw your heart in the sea with the other feathers,

and watch it float,
knowing the anchor of love is nothing but a sly grenadine
in a pail of water.

Broken brown

I jumped off the cliff for a dare, or maybe it
was love, or some grotesque rehash,
like Frankenstein, monster love.

I was a child in chains wondering if love
was a breakdown,

rendering you still, numb and always waiting
by the phone.

It was not like the moment I bought a drill,
or thought about drinking cups of bleach.

This was different, this was love. I knew it
because as I fell I felt the wind underpin my

shoes,
as if it was turning back the tide, reeking of
manure

yet salted as sea, swaddling my mantled
cheeks.

As I hit the ground then it blustered into
fury, whipped the sky blank and scudded

birdsong to the tree. The pain welled in a
tight ill-fitting shoe, my tissue torn but

that wasn't the same as when I bought the
borer.
That day the rain lashed as if gnawing on
bone.

The sky came on like a river wanting
to drown, to eddy out to the tune of the sea,

to whirl like the tooth of a drill.

I did it for love, I think,

I did it because there was nowhere left
to run,

with a pallid sun in the sky, beating wind, onset
of rain, just another autumn

but then a snap on the grass, a pillow of
leaves changing from green
to broken brown.

Cow fleeing in spring

It was on their pasture with my snow boots in
the rifts of mud cakes,

on this tract of farmland and slow rolling
mountain, an overbite hanging with the
precariousness of infant teeth.

It was stone in the eye, but also hurt, as though
violated, and I was awash with guilt

for this was trespass.

Then we hurried toward the latch, sun painting
the skyline dull orange, mashed fruit setting
in the nape of hill,

grey marsh bickering in the gutter of trees,

but I won't take your hide for leather, or draft
you to the plough turning soil,

and the grazing wait for rainfall, then dapple the
land in spots of water,

sunder at the eyes when the heifer
and the calf moo,

but I won't take your bones for the machine,
or rip out the fourfold stomach, lift your milk.

I can hear the lowing in my sleep,
delivered as a hymn on the green,
that low moan from a death in the shadows.

As we near the gate I hear the shooing in her
voice, it is loud enough for the post

and we run away in silence
leaving the bulls to roam in their hoofed strut,

cud chewing at the mount of the land.

Nothing left to say

It has become an ice walk, with snap of skin
over water, has the fear of losing it like tears
falling through the snow.

If it disappears completely, as balloon punctures
to collapse, it is lost and terminal among the
brambling,

the bag of chips beside the tracks,

the sugary, winy tongue that erupts at the mere
thoughts,

gatherings at the brow house where paper was
root of all imagination.

When it is gone can I drink the water of
Mnemosyne, sit upon the chair and recount all
that I do not know anymore?

I have to slip away quietly so that nobody can
tell me what I have lost to the wind, as it too
sheds its secrets like an old forest

or a dawn chorus from the nightingale.

When it is cold as the big freeze or the mount
of McKinley, shall I warm by the strangeness
of modish yarns

or feel the uncertainty of a new order?

I am too young I say, but then the wind tells
me that nobody is too young,

anything can happen these days with enough
push,

just as a fall through the skin of ice can wipe it
all out,

no yesterday anymore

no more to umpire, examine, resolve

and at last there is nothing left to say.

At the corner and then nowhere

It was at the end of sepulchre street where we saw
the stars of Frisco, gently bending to the bow of a waning
moon.

It was on the rooftop that we sank and heard the rowing
of sirens, the lighthouse that govern a piece of rock.

Then it was our land to pry open, to just watch the passing
and brood among the cru.

It was winter when we chose to forget, at the corner
we laughed then auctioned our cries,

sand upon sand we dug out a trench, kept it for our longing,
filled it with sour wine.

Then on that street the shadows left us to choose again, to
give the land back as repentance,

we ate honey and bread and the stars waxed, burst out of skins
and salted the ocean,

they were our catch, the tide told us so, they would not lie
to one whose story was mine.

We accord the sky its feather and dust, the land its master,
proffer the night with sound,

I listen for the aches, make music of its scar, tend to a rolling
tongue that cries an eternity of field hollers,

that hyaline sea that bawls.

I have the stars and moon, the secret of longing,

and it was at the end of sepulchre street
that we learned of loss.